mArshMaLLOWS & dESPair

dAvid ossMan

NeoPoiesisPress.com

ℛ

NeoPoiesis Press, LLC

2775 Harbor Ave SW, Suite D, Seattle, WA

For more info: Info@NeoPoiesisPress.com

David Ossman – Marshmallows & Despair
ISBN 978-0-9903565-7-8 (pbk)

　　　1. Poetry. I. Ossman, David. II. Marshmallows & Despair.

Library of Congress Control Number: 2015937516

First Edition

Design, art direction and typography: Milo Duffin and Stephen Roxborough
Cover illustration: David Ossman
Author's photo: Rocky Schenck

Printed in the United States of America

Again, and always, for the children.

Acknowledgments

Some of these poems I first read on Peter Bergman's weekly "Radio Free Oz" webcast during 2010 and 2011 and a few were first printed in the anthology *Trolling The Woe*, published shortly after Peter's death in March 2012.

A few of these poems were included in *Fools & Death*, published by Ion Drive in 2010. "Cell Phone Nightmare" appeared in *Dr. Firesign's Follies*, Bear Manor Books, 2008. "Brentwood Haiku" and "Beverly Cul-de-Sac" first appeared in *Milk 2-3*.

Beat St. Jack's raps ("raps" in Peter Bergman's sense of a hiply surreal editorial) were created for Firesign Theatre's "Fools In Space" series on XM Satellite Radio (2000-2001) and Firesign's frequent 2001 broadcasts on NPR's "All Things Considered."

Some were also performed at Lit Fuse, Tieton WA; Beyond Baroque, Venice CA; Burning Word, Greenbank Farm, WA; Whidbey Island Center For The Arts, Langley WA and the Ott & Murphy Wine Cabaret, also in Langley.

By those notes, it can be seen that the work in this collection has been written over the first 15 years of the 21st century, a lot of it while working far away from home. As 2014 ends, the daily news that provokes poems of anger or sadness continues with numbing frequency. For this reason, and because my hope for the future is in our children, I've ended this collection with prayers in place of rants.

A thank you is gratefully extended to *The New York Times* for its frequent editorial inspiration.

". . . an America we all wish we lived in, where the pigs are fat and healthy instead of lean and terrifying, and yams taste of the earth and the sky, not marshmallows and despair."

Sam Sifton, NYTimes

Contents

Three – Home In America

Four – Seeking Refuge

1 *FLIGHT PATH*

Big Bald idles in the sky
Breezes curl the tresses of the trees
Harbor idly bares its beaches
Two Grays surface together off the Ferry
Sun long gone
A rattler   A pusher
A fistful of wind

Presidential Butts in Butter!

Once again, for the flavored few,
the New World Mint trots out:
a delectably collectable selection of
six handsomely hand-molded Chief Executive Posteriors
in Pure 24K oil-fed Creamery Butter.

Purchase your Personal "Thank You Mr. Presidents" Prize
Package right away today and we'll bend over the Moon
to show you a 4-cheeks-for-2 New World Deal you can have
as long as they last!

That's right! We'll ship out your very first sofa-size
send-up of our New World Mint Julius and self-tossed Caesar -
the Dubya Bush Junior Butter Butt with a slick, kissable
Texas Cook-Out Finish in Pretzel Tan
that smirks like a million points of friendly fire!

Then, chose your choice of Dads!
Try out the un-loveable loser of the Un-ited Un-evil Um-pire,
the Lesser Elder George H. W. Bush Butter Butt!
Some folks think that a daily fat pat on a tight Bush
brings fortunes to lucky fingers fast - and on the Inside.

Or why not pick on the prick-ly ex-People's Choice!
Exxx-press yo-self, Pops, with the Hop On Pop Prexy's coxyx
sent frozen in Fed Ex's ex-truck and Extra Finely struck out:
The way you'll always want to think about watching him.
Laid low and inside.   Spread wide.
Suitable for gettin' framed.
Kiss up today! To Presidential Butts in Butter!
From the New World Mint,
where our wildest dreams are made of fat.

Infrathin Politics/Infrathin Pain

1. Margin of Error

I haven't had anyone say I pushed at it
and couldn't get it out

> Our standard is at least two corners need to be broken
> in order to be a vote

It's razor close
and the margin of error
is bigger than the margin between them

> minimally elevated level
> hinged on a hanging chad

2. The Butterfly Ballot

> "I saw people scattered on the ground,
> people without limbs."

"I think it lends credibility to the election process."

> A deep ache, a burning pain, sharp jabs,
> an electric shock

"For us the main determinant was cost."

3. The Ozone Layer

a slight change in temperature
    the brush of hair against skin
        slow emissions of heat-trapping greenhouse gasses

        a windfall of pollution credits
    loopholes would prevent cuts
wiping whipped cream from his lip

4. Slays Self and Family

"I think that I was gripped   by the hope   of one more shot
      I did not know   how else   to escape   what
I got myself   into.   It   is   over."

5. Longevity

        "God has been
        good to me. I've
        never smoked,
        drank or dissipated."

        Isabella Doyle of Everett,
        who turns 105 on Friday.

Thanksgiving 2000
Everett, WA Herald

The Engrossing Questions of the Day

A grave indictment of independent citizenship

A flagrant offence against public opinion

A blaze of popular resentment

Political fakery

Blind partisanship

Signs of a genuine awakening in the Nation

A shifty self-seeking politician

A corrupt public sentiment

An unfortunate deadlock

Facts officially winked at

These recriminations go on forever

It is regarded as a mere eczema on the body politic

From Putnam's Handbook of Expression
Birthday Poem 12.6.2000

Famous Accountants School!

[Beat St. Jack's First Trance Rap, 2001]

Gone, gone, gone is the 20th century,
when accounting was a drab and nerdy occupation
for The Little Guy!
Now! The lid is off!
The votes are in! There's . . .
Famous Accountants School!

Learn to drive the big stealer-dealers!
Sales-tax evasion, off-shore loansharking,
multiple cokehead re-entry bookkeeping.
Cook books!
Spend bucks!
Click here now!

Incorpor-pirate in a warmer climate
before it gets too hot at home.
Haggle in the Infrathin! Trade Interstate Emissions,
Hedge Gas Futures, a virtual balance sheet renter be!
Get out of the Pit and get onto the Pendulum!
It's all thrills! It's a Closed Course and
you're a Trained Driver
at Famous Accountants School!

No one turned down! Confidentially assured!
Change your life today!
Get all the perks, benefits, stock options
and admiration from your fellow men
that comes with a high-floor multi-national partnership
and a secure and immediate fiscal retirement plan.
Stop being a Mark! Learn Mark-to-Market Electrical
Three-Prong Monte!
At Famous Accountants School!

Click here now!
No tests, no classes, no books or interviews.
Click here now!

Our skilled instructors have evaded prosecution
for white-collar crimes and soft political payoffs for decades!
Jump over the Bright Line.
Click here now!
Win your personal race to the Bottom Line!
Click here now!

Restate your revenue over and over and over again
every time you slide like rawhide through a Legal Loophole
at
Famous Accountants School!
Click here now . . . Click here now . . .

Area of Refuge

"The Nothing that is and the Nothing
that isn't. It's here."
Judith Walcutt, Las Vegas, 1.6.2001

i.

How the dappled sky
fades not
and all is false

but
great-breasted sluts
express
the true

ii.

The porno-minded carry
fresh cigars
bright quarters
legs without end

breasts worn like
the dry ranges rising
above a plain of dry light
and
unfulfilled promises

(The Venetian)

SEN / IOR CITI / ZEN

I.

On a scale
of gloves and roses
of cut-paper tropics
of voices in chaos

    on a scale of mariachis
    on Main Street
    and tourists from Tex-Mex
    with peach margaritas
    and brand-names in neon

        balancing Union Station/
        soul food
        balancing
        flirtinis/
        flatlanders out in Saint Paul

        on
        the scales of say
        you or me
        of say
        your children vs. mine
        of say
        cutting my family out of your soon-to-be dream
        in everyone's last movie

"What the heck,"
they all said,
"What's the difference?

II.

Or let's compare
beautiful Buddhas tall as still buildings
with brokers and busboys
beautiful as Buddhas

    how about
    your past tense?
    as over against
    my future
    indicative!

        and weigh
        flags-on-parade
        against death-by-stones
        against
        the importance of beards

            now the pleasure of taking 'em out
            now the thrill of bright noise
            in the hearts of the mountains

                now in the heart of the homeland
                ceremonies of state
                fragile secrets
                and
                catch-up ball

on a scale of
the coins on your eyes
the hairs on your face
vs.
the tears in our pockets

       "What the heck,"
       they all said.
       "What's the difference?"

8 October-7 December 2001

12

Baghdad Bush Suit

Jack's back on the bully bandstand –
Got my fat black mike stuck in my hand – Let's lay it down!
Let's Click Here Now!

Gone gone gone is that Desert Storm Tan,
That wimpy eastern Desert Tan,
That early-90s fashion-style –
Camouflage panties on Vicky's secret cuties,
Sub-teen patriot gun-club get-up,
Daddy's slick duck-blind Sports Utility upholstery!

Yeah, the thrill is gone!
You bettah dress the kids right –
There's a tough new style –
A high-fashion-storm comin' down
On the backs of our boys and girls!

So let 'em model the Baggy Baghdad Bush Suit!
In a super-power mix of petroleum black,
Cut-down-pine brown,
Deep deep deficit red and
Golden Cee E Operatin' green!

You'll preen, you'll scheme!
The kids'll gleam
Like a rocket's red scare!

So Modern Moms,
Suit 'em up at home for home-front in-security.
Dress your little chicks and chums
For contingencies, collaterals and sudden changes of regime
In the Baggy Baghdad Bush Suit!

Get it on!
Operation Cloudy Crystal Ball!
One size fits all. So get it right!
Bring back the uniform,
The uniform opinion.
Dress 'em up! Dress 'em down!

Click here now.
Go it alone!
Click here now!
Don't change your mind! Click here now!

This is Beat St. Jack, tellin' you if you're Strong and Wrong
Then you better re-dress for suck-cess.
So click here now . . . Click here now . . .

The First Five Days of War
on the Last Five Days of Winter

Spring talks like a bird this morning.
We must get stoned for the war"
Anon.

ONE

On the first Day of War
clowns could still laugh just in time

There were still
48 hours
and the plums and cherry trees would still be
shedding petals
as

that Cowboy sez: "Git outta town!"
Whole Nations are ready
to fall like flesh pink petals
on the streets of Ali Baba

TWO

The second Night of War
the Full Moon exposes the Bay and flies on

The Orange alert pulses in its Safe Place
Navy aircraft pass over in the night again

and the rustling of Forces
their distant quarter-million all ears in the night

the bad Bag-daddies more awake than all of Los Angeles
the Big Man's clock ticks blindly on past 24

and you can hear the earthquake's mumble
of bombs tuned-in and excited to be moving

Heroes strive to be born and smoke or talk of
targets like boxes of chocolates to be eaten:

this Palace, that Bon-Bon, this Garden, those Thin Mints
and
Sour
Cherries

And all the time
I hear the children run
I can hear the children running

THREE

The Third Day begins with sand blowing in the Wind

Later
Preston comes out yelling
"It says War Alert! It isn't Samurai Jack!"
Instead
it's the World's
Most Dangerous Man
who's starting the War now
in front of us
because they have Fearless Leader in their sights

It's Go

And the Valley of Babylon displays its
Millions of jewels
Under yellow lamps on a slippery Euphrates night

FOUR

Our ears are shut on the Fourth Day of War

We aren't listening
and there's no information
we have no opinion
we aren't listening

FIVE

Headlines at Seven on the Fifth Day:

The Masters of War seem to hold back
    Our Bible-sized Monsters
    Mothers of All Shock 'n' Awe

And target their Telephones
    Monsters of Evil targeted
    as they're Chatting on the Verge

Embedded safely down we say:

It's like taking out just say Shrine Auditorium
or only the Kodak with some Grauman's Chinese collateral

17

only
City Hall or the D. C. Mall
and on to where their Bully Gates seal off their Comfort Zones

When do we send in Gog and Magog
or is the Garden of Eden
not the place?

17-21 March 2003

Nature at Work

First the squirrel ran
inside the shadows of a woodpile
and then
over soared
the eagle
out of a blue clear sky
pursued
by
a tempestuous
sparrow

The War follows like a pair of killer jets
scattering the oysters
shattering the ordinary day
searching out bad guys
like loud-mouthed squirrels
panicked, shivering
in a prison
of old boards

late june oh three

19

7ᵀᴴ Street Flight Path

At the Barricades of Flower
                    &
                    Hope
                    &
                    Grand
                    Darktown Chandler LA

Midnight Expressionist sidewalks
wall-to-wall
with their Nobodies and running shadows
and
surrounded
by the echoes of swift traffic

A knot of cops
drawn tight around a black-and-white
at the roots of the towers

Keeping tomorrow's
jack-in-the-box
locked down

Only here tonight
drinking cop coffee
looking like cop actors
ready to point me down the 7th Street Flight Path
toward the Sheraton
its refuge
its thick dark rugs and lobby palms
and the piano
playing all night by itself

Blackhawk Blues

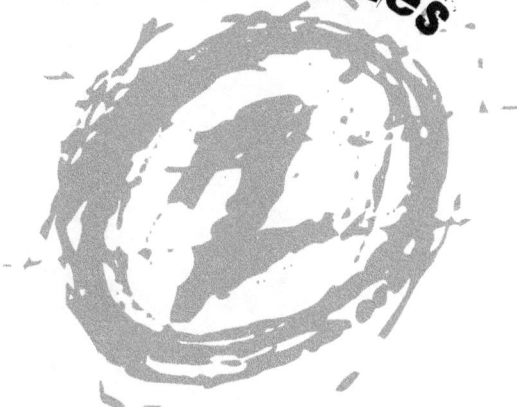

ABSORBING the information being crammed into
your skull at school,
UNDER the leaves the ground decays,
THE vote sways like a ship in a storm,
UMBRA devours the mornings,
MASQUERADES begin and end.
NEVER-the-less we go on.

Preston Ossman, 2004

Black Hawk Cellphone Nightmare

You can read while you chat while you vedge while you phone
while you eat 'cause you can from a can on the can in your van
on the lam from Black Hawks overhead in your head.

Get a grip, it's your trip, you can game while you smile
while you colon close parentheses smile,
watch DVDs in your BVDs
24/7 on line takeout in a 7-11 neon heaven
you're right at home where the Smiling Slushy Guy
who helps on the fly,
takes out each Black Hawk that's landin' in your head.

Listen in, your phone is ringin' Dragnet, it's ringin' Star Wars,
it's ringin' 8 Mile, listen Sk8erBoi, it's downloadin'
your stock market investment portfolio Happy Funds Account
while you freekin' vedge! While you duck the sneaky feelin'
you're a gamer loser gamer over under heavy fire from the
Black Hawks still circlin' in your head.

Hey, you can still sing karaoke with some Okie if you wanna
from Okefenokee to Old Smokey
on the little color screen
big as the book of matches you don't carry
'cause you're not smokin' like you used to, no sir,
you're drinkin' water from Jakarta
and jokin' on the phone to Joan, you know it's Joan
'cause there's her picture, bright as a two-billion-year-old galaxy
clear as midnight on the Tigris
there on the little screen
on the foldable phone
that rings and rings like a man in a music-box

and rings all night like a sax singin' in a subway
where you dream you're joggin' in your Vicky underwear
under where the Black Hawks keep stalkin' the last pockets
of resistance
in the wireless wonderworld of your post-war pomme-de-terre.

The Day of the Dead

I.

It came after the Chinese-pumpkin-red Full Moon
and after revelations about new-found chocolate candy skulls
of real
Little People
who, if they lived on a tropical island not far from Nowhere,
they surely must have lived
everywhere

And after the obsidian-edged museum show on Aztec bloodlust
when eating hearts
was a ritual raw-bar
of the kind a God's Top Reps like best

mas salsa?
Yum!

> After those things
> What could we expect today?

Suddenly appliances trigger false alarms! Distress signals!

  Cries for Help!   @121.5 MgH   Swift satellites

send in the EMT to rescue: a freaked-out middle-aged TV
                                  hysterical refrigerator
                                  skitzy garage door opener
                                  spastic photocopier
                                  twisted android vacuums
                                  razors with dementia
and a frantic display of outdoor Christmas lights totally
                                  on the blink

I read of battles in Zhongmou County provoking haiku like:

WHO KNEW?
In sad Zhongmou fierce
Han still kill Hui where
Winter blooms through empty skulls

By the way
Korean evangelists are working hard to make Infidels
from pious Jordanians   and I guess we think that's swell

II.

Yesterday's random architecture is today's Potemkin
as-if-there-had-been-a-yesterday façade
for brand-new theme-downtowns

[really malls]

Main Streets
of make-over
make-believe America rising out on the desert as we speak
to make over million$ off the millions who live in a million
Southern California nowheres

They say that "clone-towns" efface once half-timbered
High Streets in Jolly Old Blair-land   No,
Miss Marple will not take her tea
at Starbucks, thank you.
Not there, nor in Rancho Cucamonga!

Meanwhile in Dubai with its golden dune-buggies

and man-made islands visible from Space
billionaires air-condition
a souk twice the size of all your most naked dreams
building a billion-dollar
Somewhere
where there isn't any Where at all

III.

Noirly,
the shadow world of penny stock frauds
ejects a player

Bizarrely,
fine upstanding gas-masked and brown-briefcased Americans
grovel on the tube to please a False Boss
(and vote for one)

Others,
terrorist-Americans willing to not-really die
but metaphorically kill and truly endure
loss of face
for a greatly gilded start-up comb-over make-believe Future
trading Futures on the sleezy penny-mart

IV.

Not to mention:
    The slashed
    The poisoned
    The redecorated
    The unmothered, unfathered, unfamilied
    The un-fucked and the fucked and the

all-fucked-up all

performing like the President   confidently, tragically,
all
for the sake of faking
Our Reality

and they do it
    in the face of constant threats
        of home-made nukes,
            advancing cholesterol,
                lesbian weddings and yes,
                    the price of gas

V.

So I eat my candy skull today in memory of

#1108:
Stephen P. Downing II, age 30
PFC Army, 17th Field Artillery

and of the Red and Blue nation which put him up for death

[crunch]

And now, the heart . . .

November 1-4, 2004

R/T SEATAC/LAX

A basil and anise mist
settles an overcast of dill

The Chinese broccoli
and Walla Walla Sweets
take the air

But hair's the thing down here
where all the hills of Hollywood
impress the Bay

A face of hair
the Stars' disguise
that
and the careless silent blonde
with Oscar Night Eyes

The Galley
Santa Monica

Funny Skydiving Poems

i. Under

a tacit shell-colored
fading sky

the mood around here since
Election Day

thick & dark as old
oil

steeped in overcast

where words lose their meanings

in the mist
and in the fog of battle
everything is dust

post-mortem
death-watch

in a nation where folks
have certainly taken
leave of their senses

And to think of the Staked Plain
of Plano

ii. Re: Joyce

Vi-agra in dustbinnew pill at cheap popish
Want to start getting flussy every night?

This improbable place, pythagoras
A tadpole admidases forklift.

Milage leverage
constant flit
Doorman cottage generous
Mooney

iii. A Perfect Day w/W

i.
"I'm going to have lunch
with
Secretary of State
Rice,
talk a little business;

Mrs. Bush
talk a little business;

We've got a friend from
South Texas
here, named
Katherine Armstrong;

Take a little nap.

ii.
I'm reading an Elmore Leonard
book right now,
knock off a little more Elmore Leonard
this afternoon;

iii.
Go fishing with my man,
Barney;

A light dinner and
head for the
Ballgame.

iv.
I get to bed about 9:30 p.m.,
wake up about 5 a.m.,
so it's a perfect day."

iv. Paramount Pictures Magnet Poem

Surprise, together we lust for Gold
Money incubates ruin
Everything essential is not Popular
Shine when the time come s
Delicate whisper from Mother to Boy
"Remember

v. A Murder Passes By

The crows are listening
to Bob Dylan

A quartet
on
descending
branches
of a tall and pointy cedar

They are still on the swaying branches
and face North

The Alpha crow at the peak of the cedar sways
and some baleful squawking erupts

And Bob ain't gonna work on Maggie's Farm . . .

Two crows appear to engage in a
lengthy
kiss

    . . . five, six, they fly away   the tree is empty

vi. What The President Said & When He Said It

September 18, 1971
"To play an awful long shot,
is there a woman yet?
That would be a hell of a thing
if we could do it."

September 19, 1971
"I'm not for women in any job.
I don't want any of them around.
Thank God
we don't have any
in the cabinet."

September 30, 1971
"So,
I lean to a woman only because,
frankly,
I think at this time, John,
we got to pick up every
half a percentage point
we can.

I don't think
a woman should be in any
government job
whatever.
I mean,
I really don't.

The reason why I do
is mainly because they are
erratic
and emotional.

Men are erratic and emotional, too,
but the point is
a woman is more likely to be."

vii. Mind The Gap

Do not use words like "Fire" or "Bomb"
    in the hearing of the public.

    The code word for fire is "Mr Sands"
        and the code word for bomb is "Blackbird."

viii. Labiodental Flap

"as if a fishhook R
    had been slammed leftward
        into a lowercase v
so hard
    its vertical had merged
        with
the right leg
    of the v
        and
the dangly bit
    had been left hanging there
        like
the drain pipe out of an upstairs toilet
    in a
        partially demolished building"

ix. Far From Home (L'Envoi)

Polish driver   luminous   with language
          warms   the wet Spring night
               with Malcolm Lowry

Dimensional Discoveries

1. THEM!

Plague of tent caterpillars
inter-dimensional spawning ground
billions and billions of molecular transformations,
interactions with Up,

the falling of them off of the eves and gutters,
                    the relentless confusion crossing the road
        clustering on the mail boxes,
                            the bird-feeder roof,
            the rim of an old basket

                    squirming and transmogrifying,
                                jillions of bursts of will to eat
            and climb and search
for the Death of Form and Substance

for which they were cast upon the third dimensional
shores of our lifetime
from a still terrifying cataclysm of mass rebirth

2. SOX!

His white sox   a pair
anywhere   by the PC   in the driveway
        on top of a box
        of Summer sleep-out sheets
        that has no Winter resort

sox filthy as old potatoes wrinkled-up turkey-necks
Black Holes   where time/space bleaches out white

Unexpectedly here and there   a pair
        usually   sometimes
            a single

            smelly portal to Preston's
            Other Dimension

Slack Key Blues

How it crazed them
sailors used to using septic whores
in port-side cribs
to witness visions of brown bare breasts
cutting the foam
palm wine for air

How it crazed them
strict constructionalists
colonial Congregationalists
on their misbegotten missionary expeditions
to witness visions of damned brown breasts
denial sharp as nails
furious with sin and hula

How it crazed them
cane planters and captains of capital
petty politicians
brainless Marines in polished puttees
to witness visions of nut-brown Royals
singing to their children
so lock them in their palaces
and let the broken bones of coral
roll on the tide

The broken bones of coral
singing to the children
how it crazed them
rolling, cutting, sharp
and
fixed as bayonets
in the twilight frenzy of the tide

Heisenberg at Holmes Harbor

COLLISION WITH BIKERS!
Each a handsome silver senior guy
or leather gal, all-weather pal
like everybody I know

These unpredictable
atomic bikers
out for an azure Island afternoon
burst in like so many cosmic rays
over our transparently hydrogen harbor

A mesonic interaction
of entirely separate chemical nuances
and
like everybody I know
full of the weak force
or full of the strong force
and speaking the language of gravity
positive
or negative

The random percussion of visiting bikers
and my own infinite possibilities
exchanged at a distance
various atoms
and "Have a good ones"
and unfamiliar vapors
and everybody
spoke the language of memory

And continued right out on track
right on through
Everything
and like everybody I know
onward toward

Nothing

Spies

Stazzi Goon Squads
measure
the infra-thin evi-dence of treach-ery
by breath-ing through key-holes

Re-capture hate left scuffed into carpet
by the soles of innocent shoes

And the breaths of   thoughts of   art

Squeezed from stolen webs of careful conversation
over sticky telephones

And after solitary years in stained
glass prisons
like pickles
or luckless spiders
pig's knuckles
or hunks of careless autopsy

Some bitter smells do grow and bloom
inside these bottles

Break out

And over-
throw
a politics
of stale intelligence
and
sour breath

Sundowning

Cascading mountains strip a ragged edge from the sky
swollen orange
with sundown

stripped themselves
of cloud, fog, storm
even of a decent haze over the rainforest

and sundown comes
hunting for old ladies
sundown roams the halls
punishing old ladies

with dim dreams of maybes
the barely awake of nevermind
nightfall of why am I here

but sundown has no answers
just
sinks its teeth into the pale green skin of the day

old ladies listening
carefully shuffling toward night
hear this
and the tearing sound is only the mountain tops
slowly leaving the sky

For my mother, Jordan, 98

3/16/08 – "Freedom is a gift from God"

*"Removing Saddam Hussein was the right decision
early in my presidency, it is the right decision now,
and it will be the right decision ever."*
– GWB Ides of March 2008

I.

As Winter ends, one of those damn construction
                              Long-armed construction
                                             cranes
                                             came
                                             crashing

crushing
down on some poor 51st St. brown
stone
some   scattered   cars
        all over the Avenue   four dead
        collateral damage   for condos

I might have been walking with my youngest son to Starbucks
Simply walking by
from our apartment
half-a-block   away

II.

" . . . we blundered into an ill-conceived occupation
that would facilitate a deadly insurgency from which we
and the Iraqis are only now emerging . . .
I had badly underestimated the administration's capacity
to mess things up."

Richard Perle, OpEd NYT

Are your boots on the ground? Well,
listen to this!
     In 1973
"Nam-Land" I wrote "by 2000 a tourist paradise"
               Then
the madness pressed closer around
the killed stoners and stone killers left behind
    Today,
    please
    take
    the
    Ho Chi Minh Golf Trail!

Have
Burgers and pho   at the 18th ho-
hum hole

Ten years ago no one knew what golf was

    said Mr. Puchalski on-the-green in the former Saigon

Ten years ago, you'd be arrested for talking about your money

III.
3/17/08 Monday

    " . . . But what about the mistaken assumptions that remain
    unexplained?"   Danielle Pletka, OpEd NYT

Your son and my son   Mrs. O'Brien
went missing on St. Paddy's Day
Specialist O'Brien, 19

Only a dot on a Texas road
Dead in the news today
And mine
Hiding
Hiding high
High on the volcano's back

"hiker missing"

The last five days of the fifth year of war
Earth
void,
of course

IV.
19 March

"This deception twisted   twisted our priorities dangerously
     dangerously   dangerously out of whack"
     N. Fick USMC Ret.

Journal:
They found his body on Mt. Rainier. 12 Noon. I loved him so
deeply. Did he ever know?
How did he lose his courage?
Or did it come back at the end?
The hideous words we'll never know

V.

April

I saw you on the News

Yes

I'm so sorry

Thank you

We are having this conversation
      in the line over $63 worth of vegetables
and a six-pack on sale
      six weeks later

Saw me on television
      In that tight shot
      that night
      at the table
      talking about an accident

KOMO right on the story   on the island   two of them
      cameraman burdened with nightly sadnesses
She sympathetic yes, but:

      What was his mood?
      His experience on the Mountain?
      You don't think he might have been - ?

      Hoping for tears
      For some Good Tape
      And a better spot at the table

I saw you on the news

It's been snowing ever since

VI.
October

Pan de muerto y zempazuchitl
A round loaf with tears
and bunches of fluorescent marigolds
bread with crossed bones
dusted with coarse sugar
filled with orange blossoms and anise

huesos y lagrimas

3

Home in America

The opulence is unbelievable
imagine purple trees
drooping roses big as Death
the view hand-made

Resurrection in Minnesota

In a nation of Monopoly Houses
Jessie owns Boardwalk
We get to pass Go

Spring illuminates the elms
broadcasting birdsong
into the flightpath

Small house of dirt-colored brick echoes
unrhythmical basketball boy
I guess we don't like him

Ancient lovers converge
to eat and drink and remember
the summers they went naked

A fine Dixie River snakes
through Calvin's upright children
otherwise landlocked

Delusions of sweet liberty
trouble the Captain
whose yacht has sprung a leak

Orphans-no-more
their new dad sings "ashes, ashes"
pulls them in a little wagon

We are each browned a little
each day heart-first
from the inside out

Beverly Cul-de-Sac

i.

jasmine on the wind
wind
weaving and clattering
at the tops of palms
wrapping and thrusting
at this little refuge
whipping the jasmine
in through open windows

ii.

morning
doves   a pair
pace together
scratch
at the empty edges of grass

iii.

the opulence is unbearable
imagine purple trees
drooping roses big as Death
the view hand-made
blown clean by Mexicans
the purple trees
mocking
the tropical calm

Brentwood Haiku

Like water off ducks
mind enters the city
Joins a lake without measure

Gangs circle the block
in black Beemers and 4-bys
Is there danger here?

The lamp will light
Dogs will howl out the Moon
Wind rattles songs from bamboo

Feet running past
Steady ticking of the clock
Summer is a heartbeat

Parking enforcement, then
anger, sadness
Witnessed from your balcony

Hotel Fig

Royal Noiseless silent on the 10th
    floor, waiting at the elevator doors
for Miss Lonelyhearts to write his book there,
    memoir of life on LA's Kansas City streets
named for Mexican politicos who ran the place before

Dawn finds the grey concrete of June overhead and
    underfoot and in between
the ceaseless all-night songs of a Mocker making up
    for absent sparrows and the cactus wren that lived
where the bougainvillea shades the parking lot

In the Twenties tiled lobby wailing Moroccan Mexico
    drowns the Mocker
and outside it stirs the empty aquamarine
    of a coffin-shaped pool
while across the street mourners sing farewell
    to blind King Ray Charles
still cursing the now-deposed Lakers

Olympic fire runs unexpectedly up the boulevard
    chased by the glassy red banners of global Coca-Cola
and the eager cameras of the local news

    Mocker chooses yet another songbird's song
Upstairs invisible fingers attack the Royal's keys

Neologistic Poems
4/27/10
"try to use each new word in a poem"

1.
"shadow banks"

big fish swallow little fish swallow skeeters
blood-suckers
in the snugaries of shadow banks
back-water eddies
dank pools off Wall Street deep
under the greenbacks and money trees
where
if you fish
they'll take your bait

2.
"malware"

serves our anxiety
spoons out ones and noughts
forks the once-singular path
knifes our lifelines
and guys named Kim
raise chopsticks
above our uncollective noodles

hey! no politics at all
can really give a nation
focus
right?

3.
"deep homology"

a little galaxy of genes
a cluster
all by themselves
could for instance create an eye
if they wanted to
these happy genes
perhaps it's their enlightened choice
to assemble spots upon a fish's back or
they could be
specialists in the semi-permeable
membrane   or not   or
depending on the eon
who can say what any
deeply
homologous
bunch of atomic bomblets in your every cell
might come up with
next since
it seems the move is theirs

4.
"captcha"

words smeared in a box on the screen
for you to figure out
if you're alive:
"completely
automated public Turing test
to tell
computers and humans apart"
thanks for the acronym
but it's a dumb game
and you can't dance to it

64

5.
"haptic interface"

your hands in 3D gloves
the lights go down
your fingers feel
they're
feeling
popcorn
salty
popcorn

the trailers roll and
it's another "Alice" and your hands
are plunging
down Rabbit's Hole
but next it's something with a solid "R"
you hold the cold hard rod in your right
as your left shoves in the clip
one more
a date-nite flick
amazing how wet
your hands become
watching stars tumble in the surf
getting to know
each other

sweating yet?
here comes the Feature
each little frame captured down your fingers
out your palm

gotta go
you can use my gloves

Rock Snot Elegy

1.
rock snot travels on felt-soled boots

the long-haired man with green eyes
blew his body right in two

got it on my phone

50 dead men all around
their blood everywhere
mingled with loose change
broken watches
bits of the "cowardly attacker"
(whichever half)
his head stuck on a fruitstand down the block

2.
rock snot keeps moving stream to stream
Southward softly
on felt-soled shoes

the over-dressed windbag with stupid hair
gets a hung jury

so goes Old Chi Town

down South in Juarez a smear
of red, white and blue blood
thickens on the pavement
policia
loitering
and a woman keens over the body whom
we'll never know

as the Drug War goes on smokin'
across some desert border grid where nothin' grows

3.
rock snot
one diatomic cell at a time
takes over
Cape Cod
one day watermelons next day slime

this guy Ramzi bin al-Shibh
doesn't look like a guy you'd trust to mow your lawn
Bugs Bunny teeth
khol-eyed, droopy lidded, stoned perhaps
on God Himself
a bad bad guy closeted in Cuba since ought-six
who
by now must know which way to face
by the arrows CIA painted on the prison floors
and surely has finished his
lessons
on how
to
apply for a job opportunity in   Yemen?

here's the thing
the CIA had that piece of rock snot in a prison
they built
in Morocco
kif capital of the World!
How did that happen? If I paid taxes I'd wonder

a bad bad Tom Cruiser of a purple plot

a make-believe Sly's still here muscle
man gun car prison human hero movie
all about this guy Ramzi from Old Shibh Town
who
didn't have a chance to go down
to the local unemployment line
and part himself piously body from soul
because like Bing and Bob the CIA could ship him off
Morocco bound

4.
That's how the rock snot moves
one long-haired green-eyed bomber at a time
one hung jury
one more body in the street
one bad bad guy
one CIA prison in Morocco at a time

one felt sole
at a time

and when you need "a break from America"
when it gets really scary around your money or your life
there's always Abu Dhabi
and the Blackwater Princes

that's where the rock snot dies
on the soles of
tough
leather
boots

from NYT 8/18-19/10

Banana Republicans

Paul Krugman says   OpEd   the Times today
         America's future is
Banana Republic   no, not the store

A nation run by Colonels like Ollie North
and the on-coming on-slaughter
of Stallone-thug wannabees so secretly
trained to kill   one-at-a-time
in this particularly bullshit war

A compassionless state
where Wall Streeter's houses are visible
from Outer Space

Slavery returns big-time to fatten,
kill, pick, clean
and I mean really clean in those 17 bathrooms
while farm rats bite the desperate hens
in the face

Rats and hens left alone with Darwin
to max-out some bottom line while
mercenary families
with choppers & whackers   guns & gasoline

make sure they can drive a truck
any damn place on God's Earth
before they barbeque for Eternity in Heaven
where it's clean

24 Sept 10

Home in America, November 2010

Goodbye, America
home of the muscle car
home of the gun

    Goodbye, America
    home to dismemberment:
    see Saw 3D and Postal 2 too

        Home of the full-body scan
        yet home to secret money
        that buys the faithful's fears

America, bigots ran you for years
the once-upon-a-time Princes
got born, shot and died

    The Colonels and Pop-Stars
    tried to run you
    but the Gun-Makers won

        So the Spies ran you for the Billionaires
        and by (Iowa) golly! Billionaires let
        the Nobodies take over

So Nobody runs you now
and the muscle-car Nation
blows a valve

    Dismembers the drive-shaft
    flattens the tires, closes the schools
    goes postal with prisons

Drives home on the rims
has a drink and sits in the car
'til we're dead

    We being America
    goodbye

Opening Day

Beener strikes Pelota
with a big wooden gavel
bigger than his head

So it appeared
in color   above the fold

Yep!   the girl's vice principal is dead
the boy's v.p. is tougher
tougher on everything

it's the military-ecclesiastical complex

Jack Webb in "The D. I."   boy!
I wanted to kill him!   how
could he talk to human beings like that?

Happens all the time
in the military-ecclesiastical complex

Everybody's an Authority Figure
back   down   over   there in DC

a Critical Mass
of Authority

a
military-ecclesiastical Mass

1/5/11

Banana Clip Republic

For Gabrielle Giffords, January 2011

down by the Borderline a guy
wants a gun a glock
goes out and gets one a grip
on glory
fully loaded

    enough big shiny bullets inside to blast
    a platoon
    of toy soldiers and reload
    on the undead

normal enough crazy guy on the Borderline
buys bullets
easy as golf-balls

get it? got it! go!

now you
are the most armed and dangerous guy
in your
Borderline barrio
at the open-carry Safeway
bulls-eye Kindergarten
side-arm Sunday School

get it? you got a vision!

carries it out like that!
like Clint would
and would have gone on gone on
          went on

          goes on

reloading
exploding like a coat full of nails
at a market in Kabul
a truckload of high-test fertilizer
outside a Starbucks

but for a slo-mo moment
when
        the reload

                slipped his grip

The House of Garden Gnomes

Welcome to the House of Garden Gnomes
where all the gnomes agree
and all are cast in gray cement
painted in cheerful Gnomish red, white and b.

Dressed up, with wigs atop their pointy hats
they chat with Pink Flamingas re: quality décor.
The ne-plus-ultra-rich invite the Gnomes for tea,
a Party, see? The pious melt when it begins to pour.

All those Garden Gnomes, when planted in their Seats,
voted once again to sack the Costal Villain Science
using Basic Garden Gnome-inomics, aka
an Open Prairie kind of open-carry-self-reliance.

Few Garden Gnomes make real dough, just petty graft.
They spend a year inside the cheerless House of Gnomes –
their paint chips off, their hats get dinged –
they'll end up at the swap-meet, clay and bones.

But over on the Senate side the Gnomes have turned,
and think they're ornamental marble knights
who sit on pedestals above our wide-eyed heads
and watch their Garden Clippers take enormous bites!

Help! The Gnomes have busted up! It's Gnome-eat-Gnome
around both Houses now! Who'll save us? Vegetables?
Root and vine and sometime boiled? Unsoiled? Let's eat!
Out in the Island sunshine where a House sans Gnome is Home.

TAKING REFUGE

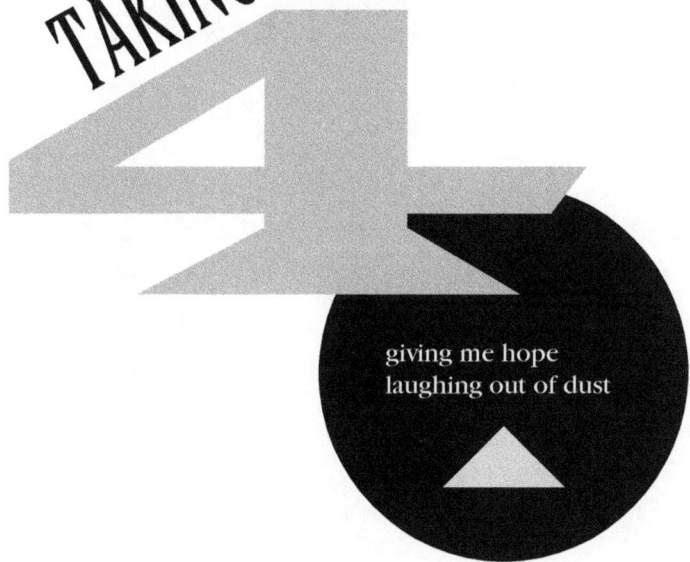

4

giving me hope
laughing out of dust

Four Refuges

i.

what the wooden Buddha contemplates
is an infinite quantity of air
reflected by an eternity of water

ii.

a room within
locks   and corridors   of doors
a shaft of air   and rain

iii.

monkey talk   and men
trimming the gardens
how shall we play today?

iv.

the Master Padmasambhava
bids me envelop the Now
in a suburban rambler

The Mind

Commendable is the taming of the mind
which is hard to hold down.
Nimble, alighting wherever it wants.
Mind subdued brings ease.

So we have made this
Mind
a thing bigger even than the bickering display
of two hungry sparrows in a sunny courtyard

Shaped Mind with noodles
and made the Great Wall of Noodles
to bring each Noodle
Peace

Left Mind
fumbling through its snapshots
of last year's
or last life's
first excursions
to the other side of a sense of itself

The Bhikkhu

Truly, a young Bhikkhu
who engages in the Buddha's instruction
this world illumines,
like the Moon set free from a cloud.

His robes
brighter than blood-
shed
golden beyond the tax-
returns
of one-percent

Answers the Bhikkhu's
question:
What do you do for fun?

He says
maybe . . .
joke . . .
giving me hope laughing out of dust

He says . . .
sleep . . .
and my son
red head on my shoulder
lotus afloat
on a shining lake of dreams

The Tulku's Birthday

Today
> sky a high-
>> altitude Catalina pottery blue
>>> pale moon
>>>> waning

Fish flying red   between the thin knives
> of the Market
>> and in the City red-with-muscle
>>> balcony barbeque

Now Master
> opens the beach stone
>> where Time hears its heart beating
>>> and birds bow their white heads

Other Work by David Ossman

The Sullen Art – Recording the Revolution in American Poetry (University of Toledo Press, 2015. Revised edition of *The Sullen Art* (Corinth Books, 1963)

The Old Man Poems (Egress Studio Press, 2015)

Set In A Landscape (lithos by Mowry Baden, el corno emplumado, 1963)

The Crescent Journals (cover by Bettye Saar, Los Angeles, 1966)

Pablo Neruda – The Early Poems, translated with Carlos Hagen (New Rivers Press, 1969)

How Time Flys – A Hi-Fi, Sci-Fi Comedy (Columbia Records, 1973)

Radio Poems: The Moonsign Book, The Rainbow Café, Hopi Set, The Day Book of The City, (1982-1984, Turkey Press, Isla Vista)

Fools & Death (Ion Drive, Los Angeles, 2009)

The Ronald Reagan Murder Case – A George Tirebiter Mystery (Bear Manor Books, 2007)

Dr. Firesign's Follies – Radio, Comedy, Mystery, History (Bear Manor Books, 2008)

Bozo Book or, Clam Calendar & Book of Ours (Turkey Press, 1981), *Anythynge You Want To, Profiles in Barbeque Sauce, Exorcism In Your Daily Life* (Bear Manor Press, 2011, 2012), *Marching to Shibboleth* (Not Insane, 2013), co-author and editor for The Firesign Theatre

Who am I anyway?

How can a poet be in two places at once? Easy. On the radio. I began broadcasting poets and poetry in 1960. In the early 70s I brought found poems to the table for the other three Firesign Theatre members and we transformed them in improvised performance. There are audio-poems in each of Firesign's many comedy albums. I've always been a political poet and those newsworthy poems have reached the world quickly over the airwaves.

I began publishing poetry in my teens, with a first collection from el corno emplumado in Mexico City in 1963. I began translating from Spanish and French in my twenties, corresponding with Jean Cocteau about "Orphée." I was drawn to the Dadaists and was able to interview one of the founders. Marcel Duchamp's objects fascinated me and I spoke to him one humbling time.

John Cage's use of chance and the I Ching, as well as his sense of the wholeness of sound in the world transformed my professional work as an audio producer as well my consciousness as a poet. NPR fired me out the door after my Sunday Show celebrated Cage's seventieth birthday. When I saw him years later he kissed me on both cheeks.

I am one of Ray Bradbury's many "sons." I've gotten "Lear" and "Titus" directly from Gielgud and Olivier. I grew up listening to Gilbert & Sullivan and Rhythm & Blues. I've collaborated with L. Frank Baum, Raymond Chandler, Dean Swift and Orson Welles. I collaborated with my Firesign Theatre partners for forty years and with my wife, Judith, more than thirty years.

My work now is to see that lifetime of works safely collected, well-selected and able to add to a resource of knowledge actually gained through experience ("I was there!") and to fresh emotions achieved through language ("You are here!").

David Ossman, Whidbey Island, February 2015

NeoPoiesis: *a new way of making*

1) in ancient Greece, poiesis referred to the process of making: creation - production - organization - formation - causation

2) a process that can be physical and spiritual, biological and intellectual, artistic and technological, material and teleological, efficient and formal

3) a means of modifying the environment and a method of organizing the self, the making of art and music and poetry, the fashioning of memory and history and philosophy, the construction of perception and expression and reality

4) an independent publisher with a steadfast goal to print and promote outstanding poets, writers and artists that reflect the creative drive and spirit of the new electronic landscape

NeoPoiesisPress.com

www.ingramcontent.com/pod-product-compliance
Lightning Source LLC
LaVergne TN
LVHW091228080426
835509LV00009B/1214